Address & Password

Keeper Book

By
Udaya Peace

Internet Website

Address .Password

Keeper Book

Published by
Udaya Peace

Record Date

Website Link

Username

Password

Note Message

Record Date

Website Link

Username

Password

Note Message

Record Date

Website Link

Username

Password

Note Message

Record Date

Website Link

Username

Password

Note Message

Record Date

Website Link

Username

Password

Note Message

Record Date

Website Link

Username

Password

Note Message

Record Date

Website Link

Username

Password

Note Message

Record Date

Website Link

Username

Password

Note Message

Record Date

Website Link

Username

Password

Note Message

Record Date

Website Link

Username

Password

Note Message

Record Date

Website Link

Username

Password

Note Message

Record Date

Website Link

Username

Password

Note Message

Record Date

Website Link

Username

Password

Note Message

Record Date

Website Link

Username

Password

Note Message

Record Date

Website Link

Username

Password

Note Message

Record Date

Website Link

Username

Password

Note Message

Record Date

Website Link

Username

Password

Note Message

Record Date

Website Link

Username

Password

Note Message

Record Date

Website Link

Username

Password

Note Message

Record Date

Website Link

Username

Password

Note Message

Record Date
_____

Website Link
_____

Username
_____

Password
_____

Note Message
_____

Record Date
_____

Website Link
_____

Username
_____

Password
_____

Note Message
_____

Record Date
_____

Website Link
_____

Username
_____

Password
_____

Note Message
_____

Record Date
_____

Website Link
_____

Username
_____

Password
_____

Note Message
_____

Record Date

Website Link

Username

Password

Note Message

Record Date

Website Link

Username

Password

Note Message

Record Date

Website Link

Username

Password

Note Message

Record Date

Website Link

Username

Password

Note Message

Record Date

Website Link

Username

Password

Note Message

Record Date

Website Link

Username

Password

Note Message

Record Date

Website Link

Username

Password

Note Message

Record Date

Website Link

Username

Password

Note Message

Record Date
Website Link
Username
Password
Note Message

Record Date
Website Link
Username
Password
Note Message

Record Date
Website Link
Username
Password
Note Message

Record Date
Website Link
Username
Password
Note Message

Record Date

Website Link

Username

Password

Note Message

Record Date

Website Link

Username

Password

Note Message

Record Date

Website Link

Username

Password

Note Message

Record Date

Website Link

Username

Password

Note Message

Record Date

Website Link

Username

Password

Note Message

Record Date

Website Link

Username

Password

Note Message

Record Date

Website Link

Username

Password

Note Message

Record Date

Website Link

Username

Password

Note Message

Record Date
Website Link
Username
Password
Note Message

Record Date
Website Link
Username
Password
Note Message

Record Date
Website Link
Username
Password
Note Message

Record Date
Website Link
Username
Password
Note Message

Record Date

Website Link

Username

Password

Note Message

Record Date

Website Link

Username

Password

Note Message

Record Date

Website Link

Username

Password

Note Message

Record Date

Website Link

Username

Password

Note Message

Record Date
Website Link
Username
Password
Note Message

Record Date
Website Link
Username
Password
Note Message

Record Date
Website Link
Username
Password
Note Message

Record Date
Website Link
Username
Password
Note Message

Record Date
Website Link
Username
Password
Note Message

Record Date
Website Link
Username
Password
Note Message

Record Date
Website Link
Username
Password
Note Message

Record Date
Website Link
Username
Password
Note Message

Record Date

Website Link

Username

Password

Note Message

Record Date

Website Link

Username

Password

Note Message

Record Date

Website Link

Username

Password

Note Message

Record Date

Website Link

Username

Password

Note Message

Record Date

Website Link

Username

Password

Note Message

Record Date

Website Link

Username

Password

Note Message

Record Date

Website Link

Username

Password

Note Message

Record Date

Website Link

Username

Password

Note Message

Record Date
Website Link
Username
Password
Note Message

Record Date
Website Link
Username
Password
Note Message

Record Date
Website Link
Username
Password
Note Message

Record Date
Website Link
Username
Password
Note Message

Record Date

Website Link

Username

Password

Note Message

Record Date

Website Link

Username

Password

Note Message

Record Date

Website Link

Username

Password

Note Message

Record Date

Website Link

Username

Password

Note Message

Record Date

Website Link

Username

Password

Note Message

Record Date

Website Link

Username

Password

Note Message

Record Date

Website Link

Username

Password

Note Message

Record Date

Website Link

Username

Password

Note Message

Record Date

Website Link

Username

Password

Note Message

Record Date

Website Link

Username

Password

Note Message

Record Date

Website Link

Username

Password

Note Message

Record Date

Website Link

Username

Password

Note Message

Record Date

Website Link

Username

Password

Note Message

Record Date

Website Link

Username

Password

Note Message

Record Date

Website Link

Username

Password

Note Message

Record Date

Website Link

Username

Password

Note Message

Record Date

Website Link

Username

Password

Note Message

Record Date

Website Link

Username

Password

Note Message

Record Date

Website Link

Username

Password

Note Message

Record Date

Website Link

Username

Password

Note Message

Record Date

Website Link

Username

Password

Note Message

Record Date

Website Link

Username

Password

Note Message

Record Date

Website Link

Username

Password

Note Message

Record Date

Website Link

Username

Password

Note Message

Record Date

Website Link

Username

Password

Note Message

Record Date

Website Link

Username

Password

Note Message

Record Date

Website Link

Username

Password

Note Message

Record Date

Website Link

Username

Password

Note Message

Record Date

Website Link

Username

Password

Note Message

Record Date

Website Link

Username

Password

Note Message

Record Date

Website Link

Username

Password

Note Message

Record Date

Website Link

Username

Password

Note Message

Record Date

Website Link

Username

Password

Note Message

Record Date

Website Link

Username

Password

Note Message

Record Date

Website Link

Username

Password

Note Message

Record Date

Website Link

Username

Password

Note Message

Record Date

Website Link

Username

Password

Note Message

Record Date

Website Link

Username

Password

Note Message

Record Date

Website Link

Username

Password

Note Message

Record Date

Website Link

Username

Password

Note Message

Record Date

Website Link

Username

Password

Note Message

Record Date

Website Link

Username

Password

Note Message

Record Date

Website Link

Username

Password

Note Message

Record Date

Website Link

Username

Password

Note Message

Record Date

Website Link

Username

Password

Note Message

Record Date

Website Link

Username

Password

Note Message

Record Date

Website Link

Username

Password

Note Message

Record Date

Website Link

Username

Password

Note Message

Record Date

Website Link

Username

Password

Note Message

Record Date

Website Link

Username

Password

Note Message

Record Date

Website Link

Username

Password

Note Message

Record Date

Website Link

Username

Password

Note Message

Record Date

Website Link

Username

Password

Note Message

Record Date

Website Link

Username

Password

Note Message

Record Date

Website Link

Username

Password

Note Message

Record Date

Website Link

Username

Password

Note Message

Record Date

Website Link

Username

Password

Note Message

Record Date

Website Link

Username

Password

Note Message

Record Date

Website Link

Username

Password

Note Message

Record Date

Website Link

Username

Password

Note Message

Record Date _____

Website Link _____

Username _____

Password _____

Note Message _____

_____

Record Date _____

Website Link _____

Username _____

Password _____

Note Message _____

_____

Record Date _____

Website Link _____

Username _____

Password _____

Note Message _____

_____

Record Date _____

Website Link _____

Username _____

Password _____

Note Message _____

_____

Record Date

Website Link

Username

Password

Note Message

Record Date

Website Link

Username

Password

Note Message

Record Date

Website Link

Username

Password

Note Message

Record Date

Website Link

Username

Password

Note Message

Record Date

Website Link

Username

Password

Note Message

Record Date

Website Link

Username

Password

Note Message

Record Date

Website Link

Username

Password

Note Message

Record Date

Website Link

Username

Password

Note Message

Record Date

Website Link

Username

Password

Note Message

Record Date

Website Link

Username

Password

Note Message

Record Date

Website Link

Username

Password

Note Message

Record Date

Website Link

Username

Password

Note Message

Record Date

Website Link

Username

Password

Note Message

Record Date

Website Link

Username

Password

Note Message

Record Date

Website Link

Username

Password

Note Message

Record Date

Website Link

Username

Password

Note Message

Record Date

Website Link

Username

Password

Note Message

Record Date

Website Link

Username

Password

Note Message

Record Date

Website Link

Username

Password

Note Message

Record Date

Website Link

Username

Password

Note Message

Record Date

Website Link

Username

Password

Note Message

Record Date

Website Link

Username

Password

Note Message

Record Date

Website Link

Username

Password

Note Message

Record Date

Website Link

Username

Password

Note Message

Record Date

Website Link

Username

Password

Note Message

Record Date

Website Link

Username

Password

Note Message

Record Date

Website Link

Username

Password

Note Message

Record Date

Website Link

Username

Password

Note Message

Record Date

Website Link

Username

Password

Note Message

Record Date

Website Link

Username

Password

Note Message

Record Date

Website Link

Username

Password

Note Message

Record Date

Website Link

Username

Password

Note Message

Record Date

Website Link

Username

Password

Note Message

Record Date

Website Link

Username

Password

Note Message

Record Date

Website Link

Username

Password

Note Message

Record Date

Website Link

Username

Password

Note Message

Record Date

Website Link

Username

Password

Note Message

Record Date

Website Link

Username

Password

Note Message

Record Date

Website Link

Username

Password

Note Message

Record Date

Website Link

Username

Password

Note Message

Record Date

Website Link

Username

Password

Note Message

Record Date

Website Link

Username

Password

Note Message

Record Date

Website Link

Username

Password

Note Message

Record Date

Website Link

Username

Password

Note Message

Record Date

Website Link

Username

Password

Note Message

Record Date

Website Link

Username

Password

Note Message

Record Date

Website Link

Username

Password

Note Message

Record Date

Website Link

Username

Password

Note Message

Record Date

Website Link

Username

Password

Note Message

Record Date

Website Link

Username

Password

Note Message

Record Date

Website Link

Username

Password

Note Message

Record Date

Website Link

Username

Password

Note Message

Record Date

Website Link

Username

Password

Note Message

Record Date

Website Link

Username

Password

Note Message

Record Date

Website Link

Username

Password

Note Message

Record Date

Website Link

Username

Password

Note Message

Record Date

Website Link

Username

Password

Note Message

Record Date

Website Link

Username

Password

Note Message

Record Date

Website Link

Username

Password

Note Message

Record Date

Website Link

Username

Password

Note Message

Record Date _____

Website Link _____

Username _____

Password _____

Note Message _____

_____

Record Date _____

Website Link _____

Username _____

Password _____

Note Message _____

_____

Record Date _____

Website Link _____

Username _____

Password _____

Note Message _____

_____

Record Date _____

Website Link _____

Username _____

Password _____

Note Message _____

_____

Record Date

Website Link

Username

Password

Note Message

Record Date

Website Link

Username

Password

Note Message

Record Date

Website Link

Username

Password

Note Message

Record Date

Website Link

Username

Password

Note Message

Record Date

Website Link

Username

Password

Note Message

Record Date

Website Link

Username

Password

Note Message

Record Date

Website Link

Username

Password

Note Message

Record Date

Website Link

Username

Password

Note Message

Record Date

Website Link

Username

Password

Note Message

Record Date

Website Link

Username

Password

Note Message

Record Date

Website Link

Username

Password

Note Message

Record Date

Website Link

Username

Password

Note Message

Record Date

Website Link

Username

Password

Note Message

Record Date

Website Link

Username

Password

Note Message

Record Date

Website Link

Username

Password

Note Message

Record Date

Website Link

Username

Password

Note Message

Record Date

Website Link

Username

Password

Note Message

Record Date

Website Link

Username

Password

Note Message

Record Date

Website Link

Username

Password

Note Message

Record Date

Website Link

Username

Password

Note Message

Record Date

Website Link

Username

Password

Note Message

Record Date

Website Link

Username

Password

Note Message

Record Date

Website Link

Username

Password

Note Message

Record Date

Website Link

Username

Password

Note Message

Record Date

Website Link

Username

Password

Note Message

Record Date

Website Link

Username

Password

Note Message

Record Date

Website Link

Username

Password

Note Message

Record Date

Website Link

Username

Password

Note Message

Record Date

Website Link

Username

Password

Note Message

Record Date

Website Link

Username

Password

Note Message

Record Date

Website Link

Username

Password

Note Message

Record Date

Website Link

Username

Password

Note Message

Record Date
_____

Website Link
_____

Username
_____

Password
_____

Note Message
_____

_____

Record Date
_____

Website Link
_____

Username
_____

Password
_____

Note Message
_____

_____

Record Date
_____

Website Link
_____

Username
_____

Password
_____

Note Message
_____

_____

Record Date
_____

Website Link
_____

Username
_____

Password
_____

Note Message
_____

_____

Record Date

Website Link

Username

Password

Note Message

Record Date

Website Link

Username

Password

Note Message

Record Date

Website Link

Username

Password

Note Message

Record Date

Website Link

Username

Password

Note Message

Record Date

Website Link

Username

Password

Note Message

Record Date

Website Link

Username

Password

Note Message

Record Date

Website Link

Username

Password

Note Message

Record Date

Website Link

Username

Password

Note Message

Record Date

Website Link

Username

Password

Note Message

Record Date

Website Link

Username

Password

Note Message

Record Date

Website Link

Username

Password

Note Message

Record Date

Website Link

Username

Password

Note Message

Record Date

Website Link

Username

Password

Note Message

Record Date

Website Link

Username

Password

Note Message

Record Date

Website Link

Username

Password

Note Message

Record Date

Website Link

Username

Password

Note Message

Record Date

Website Link

Username

Password

Note Message

Record Date

Website Link

Username

Password

Note Message

Record Date

Website Link

Username

Password

Note Message

Record Date

Website Link

Username

Password

Note Message

Record Date

Website Link

Username

Password

Note Message

Record Date

Website Link

Username

Password

Note Message

Record Date

Website Link

Username

Password

Note Message

Record Date

Website Link

Username

Password

Note Message

Record Date

Website Link

Username

Password

Note Message

Record Date

Website Link

Username

Password

Note Message

Record Date

Website Link

Username

Password

Note Message

Record Date

Website Link

Username

Password

Note Message

Record Date

Website Link

Username

Password

Note Message

Record Date

Website Link

Username

Password

Note Message

Record Date

Website Link

Username

Password

Note Message

Record Date

Website Link

Username

Password

Note Message

Record Date

Website Link

Username

Password

Note Message

Record Date

Website Link

Username

Password

Note Message

Record Date

Website Link

Username

Password

Note Message

Record Date

Website Link

Username

Password

Note Message

Record Date

Website Link

Username

Password

Note Message

Record Date

Website Link

Username

Password

Note Message

Record Date

Website Link

Username

Password

Note Message

Record Date

Website Link

Username

Password

Note Message

Record Date

Website Link

Username

Password

Note Message

Record Date

Website Link

Username

Password

Note Message

Record Date

Website Link

Username

Password

Note Message

Record Date

Website Link

Username

Password

Note Message

Record Date

Website Link

Username

Password

Note Message

Record Date

Website Link

Username

Password

Note Message

Record Date

Website Link

Username

Password

Note Message

Record Date

Website Link

Username

Password

Note Message

Record Date

Website Link

Username

Password

Note Message

Record Date

Website Link

Username

Password

Note Message

Record Date

Website Link

Username

Password

Note Message

Record Date

Website Link

Username

Password

Note Message

Record Date

Website Link

Username

Password

Note Message

Record Date

Website Link

Username

Password

Note Message

Record Date

Website Link

Username

Password

Note Message

Record Date

Website Link

Username

Password

Note Message

Record Date

Website Link

Username

Password

Note Message

Record Date

Website Link

Username

Password

Note Message

Record Date

Website Link

Username

Password

Note Message

Record Date

Website Link

Username

Password

Note Message

Record Date

Website Link

Username

Password

Note Message

Record Date

Website Link

Username

Password

Note Message

Record Date

Website Link

Username

Password

Note Message

Record Date

Website Link

Username

Password

Note Message

Record Date

Website Link

Username

Password

Note Message

Record Date

Website Link

Username

Password

Note Message

Record Date

Website Link

Username

Password

Note Message

Record Date

Website Link

Username

Password

Note Message

Record Date
Website Link
Username
Password
Note Message

Record Date
Website Link
Username
Password
Note Message

Record Date
Website Link
Username
Password
Note Message

Record Date
Website Link
Username
Password
Note Message

Record Date

Website Link

Username

Password

Note Message

Record Date

Website Link

Username

Password

Note Message

Record Date

Website Link

Username

Password

Note Message

Record Date

Website Link

Username

Password

Note Message

Record Date
Website Link
Username
Password
Note Message

Record Date
Website Link
Username
Password
Note Message

Record Date
Website Link
Username
Password
Note Message

Record Date
Website Link
Username
Password
Note Message

Record Date

Website Link

Username

Password

Note Message

Record Date

Website Link

Username

Password

Note Message

Record Date

Website Link

Username

Password

Note Message

Record Date

Website Link

Username

Password

Note Message

Record Date

Website Link

Username

Password

Note Message

Record Date

Website Link

Username

Password

Note Message

Record Date

Website Link

Username

Password

Note Message

Record Date

Website Link

Username

Password

Note Message

Record Date

Website Link

Username

Password

Note Message

Record Date

Website Link

Username

Password

Note Message

Record Date

Website Link

Username

Password

Note Message

Record Date

Website Link

Username

Password

Note Message

Record Date
_____

Website Link
_____

Username
_____

Password
_____

Note Message
_____

_____

Record Date
_____

Website Link
_____

Username
_____

Password
_____

Note Message
_____

_____

Record Date
_____

Website Link
_____

Username
_____

Password
_____

Note Message
_____

_____

Record Date
_____

Website Link
_____

Username
_____

Password
_____

Note Message
_____

_____

Record Date _____

Website Link _____

Username _____

Password _____

Note Message _____

_____

Record Date _____

Website Link _____

Username _____

Password _____

Note Message _____

_____

Record Date _____

Website Link _____

Username _____

Password _____

Note Message _____

_____

Record Date _____

Website Link _____

Username _____

Password _____

Note Message _____

_____

Record Date

Website Link

Username

Password

Note Message

Record Date

Website Link

Username

Password

Note Message

Record Date

Website Link

Username

Password

Note Message

Record Date

Website Link

Username

Password

Note Message

Record Date

Website Link

Username

Password

Note Message

Record Date

Website Link

Username

Password

Note Message

Record Date

Website Link

Username

Password

Note Message

Record Date

Website Link

Username

Password

Note Message

Record Date

Website Link

Username

Password

Note Message

Record Date

Website Link

Username

Password

Note Message

Record Date

Website Link

Username

Password

Note Message

Record Date

Website Link

Username

Password

Note Message

Record Date

Website Link

Username

Password

Note Message

Record Date

Website Link

Username

Password

Note Message

Record Date

Website Link

Username

Password

Note Message

Record Date

Website Link

Username

Password

Note Message

Record Date

Website Link

Username

Password

Note Message

Record Date

Website Link

Username

Password

Note Message

Record Date

Website Link

Username

Password

Note Message

Record Date

Website Link

Username

Password

Note Message

Record Date

Website Link

Username

Password

Note Message

Record Date

Website Link

Username

Password

Note Message

Record Date

Website Link

Username

Password

Note Message

Record Date

Website Link

Username

Password

Note Message

Record Date

Website Link

Username

Password

Note Message

Record Date

Website Link

Username

Password

Note Message

Record Date

Website Link

Username

Password

Note Message

Record Date

Website Link

Username

Password

Note Message

Record Date

Website Link

Username

Password

Note Message

Record Date

Website Link

Username

Password

Note Message

Record Date

Website Link

Username

Password

Note Message

Record Date

Website Link

Username

Password

Note Message

Record Date

Website Link

Username

Password

Note Message

Record Date

Website Link

Username

Password

Note Message

Record Date

Website Link

Username

Password

Note Message

Record Date

Website Link

Username

Password

Note Message

Record Date

Website Link

Username

Password

Note Message

Record Date

Website Link

Username

Password

Note Message

Record Date

Website Link

Username

Password

Note Message

Record Date

Website Link

Username

Password

Note Message

Record Date

Website Link

Username

Password

Note Message

Record Date

Website Link

Username

Password

Note Message

Record Date

Website Link

Username

Password

Note Message

Record Date

Website Link

Username

Password

Note Message

Record Date
Website Link
Username
Password
Note Message

Record Date
Website Link
Username
Password
Note Message

Record Date
Website Link
Username
Password
Note Message

Record Date
Website Link
Username
Password
Note Message

Record Date

Website Link

Username

Password

Note Message

Record Date

Website Link

Username

Password

Note Message

Record Date

Website Link

Username

Password

Note Message

Record Date

Website Link

Username

Password

Note Message

Record Date

Website Link

Username

Password

Note Message

Record Date

Website Link

Username

Password

Note Message

Record Date

Website Link

Username

Password

Note Message

Record Date

Website Link

Username

Password

Note Message

Record Date

Website Link

Username

Password

Note Message

Record Date

Website Link

Username

Password

Note Message

Record Date

Website Link

Username

Password

Note Message

Record Date

Website Link

Username

Password

Note Message

Record Date
_____

Website Link
_____

Username
_____

Password
_____

Note Message
_____

_____

Record Date
_____

Website Link
_____

Username
_____

Password
_____

Note Message
_____

_____

Record Date
_____

Website Link
_____

Username
_____

Password
_____

Note Message
_____

_____

Record Date
_____

Website Link
_____

Username
_____

Password
_____

Note Message
_____

_____

Record Date

Website Link

Username

Password

Note Message

Record Date

Website Link

Username

Password

Note Message

Record Date

Website Link

Username

Password

Note Message

Record Date

Website Link

Username

Password

Note Message

Record Date

Website Link

Username

Password

Note Message

Record Date

Website Link

Username

Password

Note Message

Record Date

Website Link

Username

Password

Note Message

Record Date

Website Link

Username

Password

Note Message

Record Date

Website Link

Username

Password

Note Message

Record Date

Website Link

Username

Password

Note Message

Record Date

Website Link

Username

Password

Note Message

Record Date

Website Link

Username

Password

Note Message

Record Date

Website Link

Username

Password

Note Message

Record Date

Website Link

Username

Password

Note Message

Record Date

Website Link

Username

Password

Note Message

Record Date

Website Link

Username

Password

Note Message

Record Date
_____
Website Link
_____
Username
_____
Password
_____
Note Message
_____

_____

Record Date
_____
Website Link
_____
Username
_____
Password
_____
Note Message
_____

_____

Record Date
_____
Website Link
_____
Username
_____
Password
_____
Note Message
_____

_____

Record Date
_____
Website Link
_____
Username
_____
Password
_____
Note Message
_____

_____

Record Date
Website Link
Username
Password
Note Message

Record Date
Website Link
Username
Password
Note Message

Record Date
Website Link
Username
Password
Note Message

Record Date
Website Link
Username
Password
Note Message

Record Date

Website Link

Username

Password

Note Message

Record Date

Website Link

Username

Password

Note Message

Record Date

Website Link

Username

Password

Note Message

Record Date

Website Link

Username

Password

Note Message